AGAINST THE ELEM[ENTS]

WATER

HAZEL RICHARDSON

W
FRANKLIN WATTS
LONDON • SYDNEY

This edition published in 2000

Designed and produced by
Aladdin Books Ltd
28 Percy Street
London W1P 0LD

ISBN 0 7496 2787 5 (hardback)
ISBN 0 7496 3889 3 (paperback)

First published in Great Britain in 1998 by
Franklin Watts
96 Leonard Street
London EC2A 4XD

Printed in Belgium

Editor
Simon Beecroft

Design
David West
CHILDREN'S BOOK DESIGN

Designer
Flick Killerby

Illustrator
Mike Saunders, Aziz Khan, Alex Pang,
Guy Smith and Ian Thompson

Picture Research
Brooks Krikler Research

Original concept by
Wilgress B. Pipe

A CIP catalogue entry for this book is available
from the British Library.

The author, **Hazel Richardson**, is a former
research scientist and teacher who now works as
a science writer and editor.

The consultant, **David Pedgley**, is a Vice President
of the Royal Meteorological Society, London.

CONTENTS

Introduction

Water has been both worshipped and feared: it is essential for life, but causes natural disasters through floods and storms.

In ancient times, water was seen as one of the four elements which, along with fire, air and earth, formed the building blocks for all things on Earth. Over two thirds of the Earth's surface is covered with water. Most of it is in seas and oceans, which are home to a wide variety of animals (*right*, whales). Less than one per cent is the fresh water needed for drinking and growing crops.

Yet, water can be a destructive power. Millions of people around the world suffer from monsoon rains, river floods, tropical storms and raging seas. Such dangers have forced people to divert and hold back water, by building dams, dikes and flood barriers. But when its full force is unleashed, nothing can stop this raging element. Cities are at the greatest risk from floods, as their paved streets prevent water from draining away. In major disasters, the emergency services are stretched to the full. They use boats, and also helicopters to rescue people from the tops of buildings, and to throw ropes for people to cling to.

WRATH OF THE GODS

In mythology, Poseidon was the Greek god of the sea. The Romans called him Neptune. During the Trojan War, he helped the Greeks by starting storms that sank ships. When the Trojans failed to pay him after he had helped them to build Troy's city walls, he sent a terrible sea monster to ravage the land.

THE WATER CYCLE

When water falls as rain, some of it flows down rivers towards the sea and some is soaked up into the earth, and also ends up in the sea. Eventually, it all passes back into the atmosphere to form clouds.

If too much rain falls, most of it cannot drain away quickly enough and the rivers become over-filled causing floods.

SEA CENTRES AND WAVE POWER

In undersea centres (left), people can observe the wonders of the deep without having to get wet. Water is also used to provide energy. Ocean thermal energy conversion (OTEC) provides energy through the temperature difference between surface water and deep water. Air bags or floats are also used to harness wave-energy.

In areas where the land is liable to flood, some people live in houses on stilts.

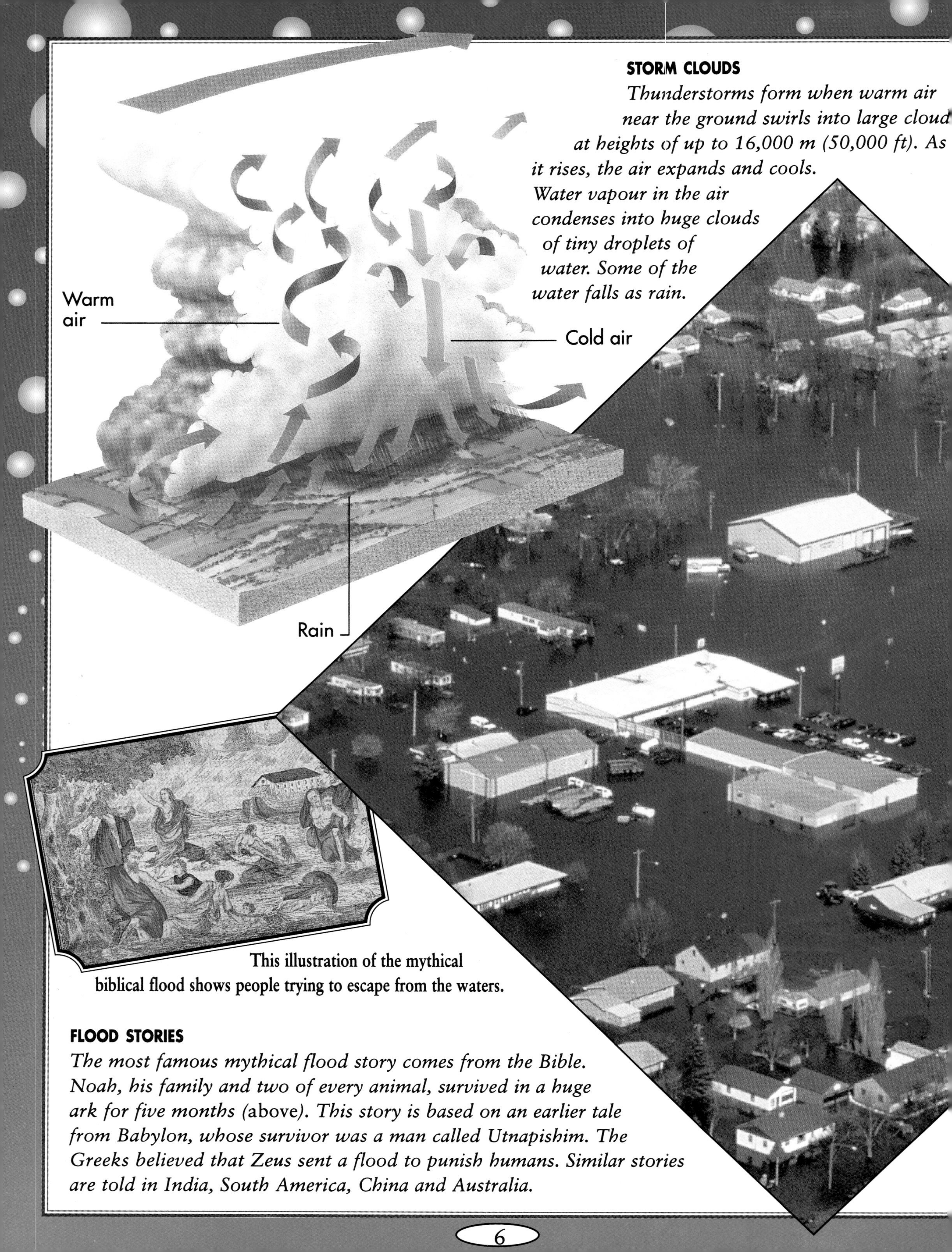

STORM CLOUDS

Thunderstorms form when warm air near the ground swirls into large cloud at heights of up to 16,000 m (50,000 ft). As it rises, the air expands and cools. Water vapour in the air condenses into huge clouds of tiny droplets of water. Some of the water falls as rain.

This illustration of the mythical biblical flood shows people trying to escape from the waters.

FLOOD STORIES

*The most famous mythical flood story comes from the Bible. Noah, his family and two of every animal, survived in a huge ark for five months (*above*). This story is based on an earlier tale from Babylon, whose survivor was a man called Utnapishim. The Greeks believed that Zeus sent a flood to punish humans. Similar stories are told in India, South America, China and Australia.*

FLOODED TOWNS

*In June 1994, torrential rains flooded a dozen cities and towns in southeastern United States. Many people drowned, and houses, cemeteries and fields of crops were washed away. These dogs (*below*) are lucky survivors.*

WHERE DID THAT HOTEL GO?

*In 1993, a hotel in Scarborough, a seaside town in the north of England, slipped into the sea when the cliff it was standing on collapsed. Scientists know why it happened: part of Britain is sinking into the North Sea. Like all the other countries in the world, Britain sits on a moving plate of the earth's crust. This plate is tilting downwards by 4 mm (1/8 in) every year (*right*) and, as it tips, parts of the east coast of Britain are being worn away by the sea, wind and storms.*

Floods

"I will bring a flood of waters upon the earth: everything that is on the land shall die."

God's words in the Bible

Over just a few days, relentless rain can submerge whole towns. 'Flash floods' are even more terrifying because of the speed at which they happen. In storms, torrential rain can flood normally calm rivers in under 30 minutes. This is not surprising when a raindrop can measure 1 cm (1/2 in) in diameter and a hailstone up to 10 cm (3 in) in diameter!

Water is heavy and, when it is moving at great speed, it becomes a battering ram that can sweep whole houses along in its path. Cars can also become death traps. Witnesses report hearing screams for help above the roar of flood waters, but are often powerless to help victims trapped inside cars. In flooded areas, people often use boats or rafts to get away from their homes (*above*).

The battle against flooding is fought by building effective barriers and by forecasting floods before they happen so the area can be evacuated. But, emergency warnings often come too late, or people refuse to abandon their homes. Floods don't just cause drowning. Mud and broken sewage pipes contaminate drinking water, causing disease to spread and, without aid, many people starve.

Floods devastate towns and cities (*above*). Power lines and gas mains break and cause fires which are hard for fire services to reach on flooded roads.

River floods

"The surging water annihilated everything in its path." ***Description of Big Thompson flood, 1976***

1 A young river

2 Broad valley

3 Flood plain

A young river carves out a channel, picking up silt as it goes (1). Over time, its path broadens the valley, and silt raises the valley floor (2). Eventually a flood plain develops (3).

In 1976, an enormous storm dropped around 25 cm (10 in) of rain onto the Big Thompson River in Colorado, United States, in as little as four hours. The flood waters rushed down the river canyon, sweeping away roads, cars, trees and even a power station. The torrent broke up the road surface, sending huge chunks up into the air. It was difficult for the emergency services to get close enough to help people and at least one ambulance was knocked off the road by the water. Helicopters were brought in to pick up the survivors. It took months for the army to clear all the wreckage using large tractors.

River floods are most dangerous in canyons or down mountains. The extra water hurtles along until it hits open land which is where people often live (*above,* a man struggles in a flood in China).

FLOOD APPEAL

*Flood waters are very destructive. Although it is hard to believe, the force of just 15 cm (6 in) of fast-moving water can knock people off their feet and cars can be easily swept away in just 60 cm (2 ft) of moving water (*left*). Aid agencies, which help in worldwide disasters, advise drivers to turn back if they come across shallow flood waters. If the waters are rising rapidly, drivers are advised to leave their cars and to climb to higher ground.*

A car is swept away by a river flood in the village of Vaison-La-Romaine in the South of France.

A MUDDY ESCAPE

*Getting caught in muddy flood waters is a harrowing experience as this struggling man in China discovers (*below*). When rivers flood, they carry tonnes of mud, rocks and plants along at high speed. It is difficult to wade through flowing water and easy to drown in the muddy torrents of river floods.*

Flood in China, July 1992 (*above*)

'CHINA'S SORROW'

The Yellow River in China is known as 'China's sorrow' because, in over 3,500 years, it has killed more people than any other feature on Earth. It has a system of protective dikes to hold back flood water but often these give way and need to be repaired. Rocks and plant stalks are dropped in nets to block escaping water.

Bundles of rocks and plant stalks

HALTING THE FLOW

*Sandbags are one of the most effective ways of trying to prevent a flood (*below*). When floods seem likely to happen, workers, and sometimes the army, pile up the bags on river banks and around houses. The bags provide a barrier against slower waters, but cannot stop very heavy floods, which simply push the bags over.*

HYDROELECTRIC DAMS

*Dams control the flow of rivers in order to prevent flooding or drought, and to generate electricity (*above*, Glen Canyon Dam). A huge lake, or reservoir, forms behind the dam and this water turns turbines to create electricity known as hydroelectric power. The reservoir also provides a water supply for irrigation and drinking. In some cases, old villages lie beneath the water (*below*) – they were evacuated first!*

Glen Canyon Dam, at the Grand Canyon in Arizona, United States, controls the raging waters of the Colorado River.

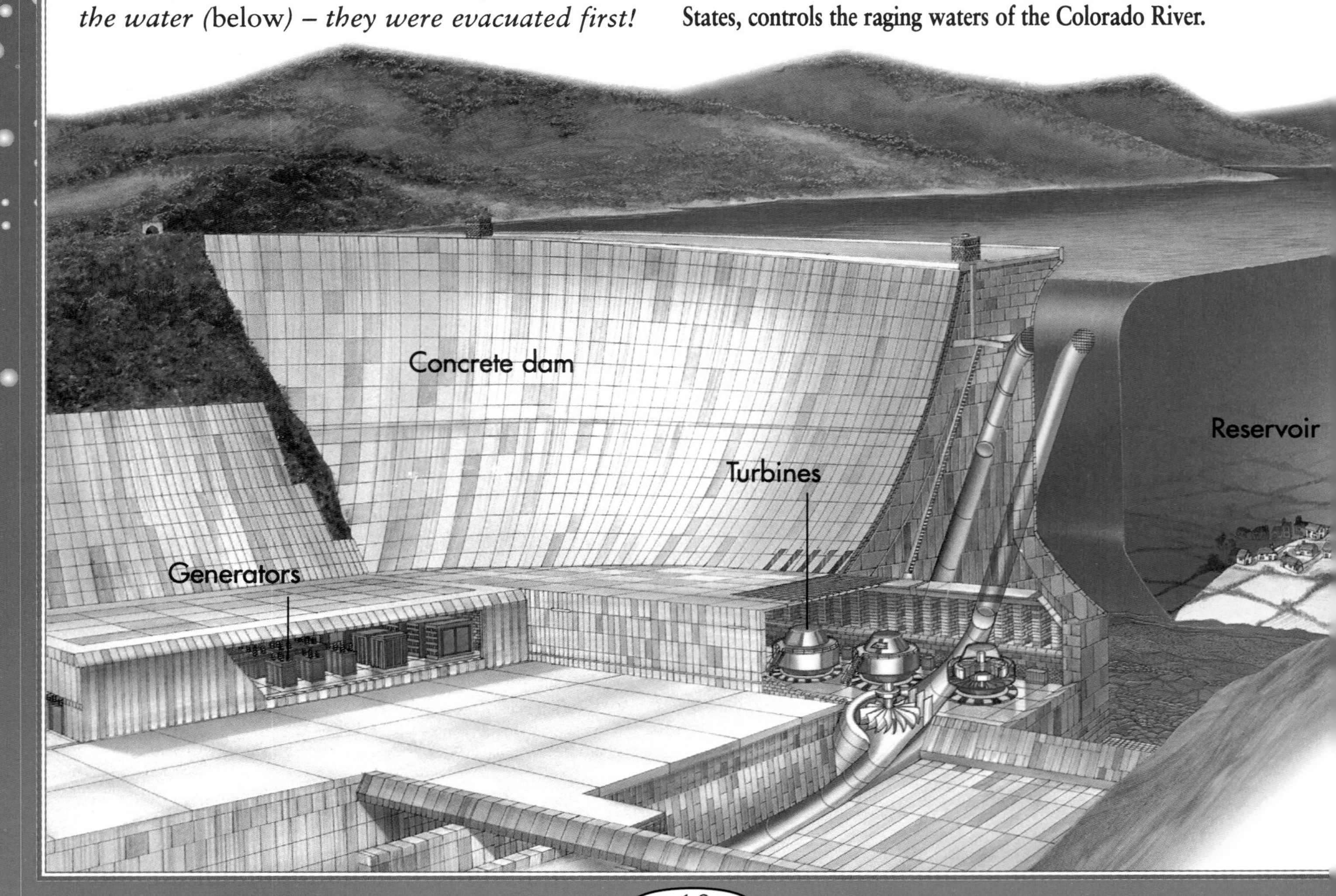

DUTCH DIKES

*In 1953, hurricane-force winds of over 160 km/h (100 mph) blew huge waves over Holland's sea walls. Most of this north-west European country lies below sea-level and, at high tide, 40 per cent of the land would flood if it was not protected by hundreds of miles of dikes and dams. Many people were caught unawares by the flood. One man lay on his kitchen table as his house flooded: he was found alive the next day, floating just beneath the ceiling. Holland's dikes also broke after heavy storms in 1775 (*left*).*

National guardsmen and volunteers in the United States are busy at work shoring up this river with sandbags to protect surrounding lands against flooding.

Dam-busters

"The gates slowly opened, and an enormous wall of water came towards us." ***Eye-witness, Florence, Italy, 1966***

Dams hold back such vast amounts of water that a failure can cause terrible floods. Failure usually results from neglect, poor design, or earthquake damage. When a dam bursts, an overpowering surge of water is released downstream which destroys everything in its path.

At exactly 7:26 a.m. on 4 November 1966, every electric clock in the city of Florence in Italy stopped. There was no power for the next 24 hours, and all communication with the outside world was severed. The worst storms in Italy for 1,000 years had caused the river Arno in Florence to flood (*above*).

The operators of a hydroelectric dam 46 km (29 miles) upstream should have gradually released rainwater as it built up. Instead they waited until the strain on the dam gates was so immense that they were forced to open them at once. Within minutes, the city was under 2 m (6 ft) of water. The ancient sewer system broke up and waste was forced out of manholes all over the city. Helicopters were drafted in to airlift survivors from rooftops, and rescue workers were brought in from other countries to assist. The extent of the disaster caused 5,000 people to lose their homes and inflicted severe damage on many of Florence's priceless works of art.

Fatal tides

"After 12 freezing hours stranded at sea, the sight of the lifeboat was like a miracle." ***Survivor of shipwreck, North Sea, 1988***

In Britain alone, coastguard services receive about 5,000 calls a year. Coastguards monitor shipping activity and are usually the first to call out naval or air rescue services. A usual lifeboat crew consists of between five and seven people whereas inflatable lifeboats are crewed by just two or three. Around 1,500 lives are saved every year by volunteer lifeboat crews.

Many distress calls come from people caught unawares by an incoming tide or by waves which suddenly crash onto the shore, leaving them cut off and stranded on rocks or in a bay.

Some of the stranded attempt to swim to shore which can end in disaster as strong tidal currents can carry a person further out to sea. Once a person becomes cold and wet, there is a risk of hypothermia – a potentially fatal condition in which the body temperature drops well below normal. Often, the first task of a rescuer is to wrap the survivor in warm blankets to help raise the body temperature.

With the growing popularity of watersports, the number of emergency call-outs increases. In open seas, currents can wash small boats way off course. Here, US coastguards rescue a group of refugees from Haiti, whose boat had been washed off course (*left*).

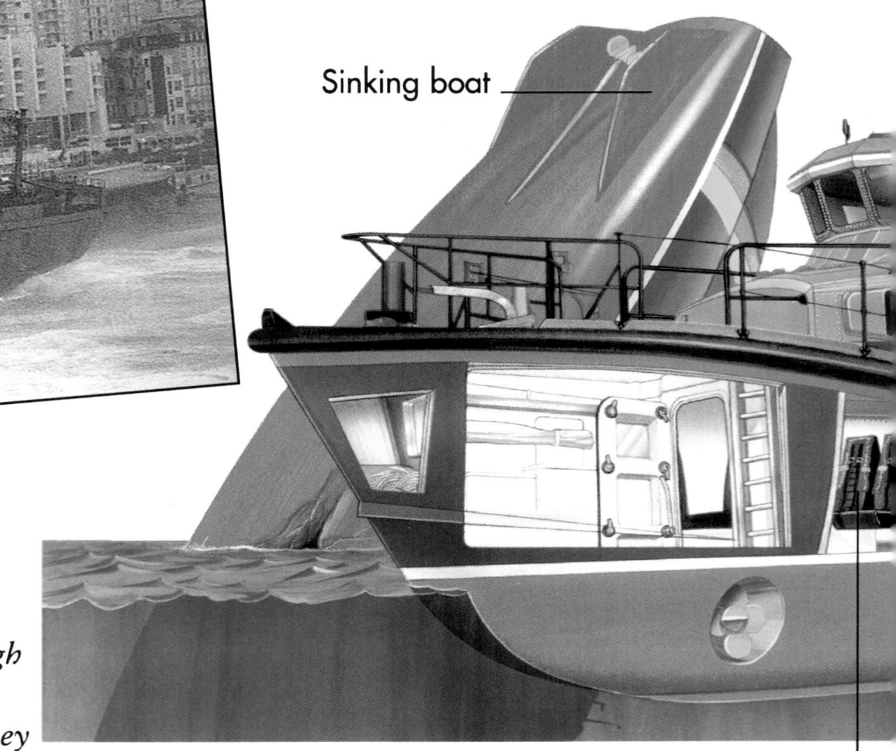

SEA RESCUE

*Because most sea rescues take place in dangerous seas, with high winds and waves (*above*), lifeboats are specially designed to skim over the surface of high waves and to right themselves automatically if they capsize (*right*). They use their satellite navigational equipment to find their way in bad weather.*

When waves break on the shore with violent force, they can easily sweep people away.

WAVE AFTER WAVE

*Waves are ripples on the surface of the sea. The water molecules in the sea get the energy to move from the wind. They move up and down in circles. The energy of each wave passes to the molecules in the next area of water, so although the waves move along, the sea doesn't (*above right*).*

n the 1954 film *The Cruel Sea*, set during World War II, allied sailors were left to rown or drift in dinghies after their ships were sunk by German submarines (*right*).

Tugboats (*left*) are sturdy boats used to rescue stranded ships at sea.

ATTENTION ALL SHIPPING!

*Weather forecasting is very important at sea. Where warm and cold air meet at fronts (*right*), storms can develop, which can spell disaster for any ships in the area. The weather over the large oceans is carefully monitored by satellites orbiting in space and by the ships in the sea. Weather planes, like this one (*below*), are mostly used for research. The strange shaped nose carries sensitive measuring equipment used to record wind speeds, air temperature and the amount of water in the air (its humidity).*

STORM WARNING

*In storms (*above*), boats may be blown off course, or into rocks or icebergs. Huge waves crash over the decks, sweep crew overboard and flood engine rooms, leaving boats stranded. Smaller boats may capsize and sink.*

CAPE... FEAR
*Cape Horn, at the southern tip of South America, is feared by sailors as the most dangerous corner of the world. Waves reach great heights, and there is an ever-constant threat of icebergs and of crew members freezing to death. For small boats, these are still the most dangerous waters to sail in (*left*).*

Rough seas

"Some waves are just too big for a small ship, even with the most experienced sailors." ***Yachtsman at Cape Horn***

Since people first took to the open seas, they have risked disaster from high waves and winds, fog, hidden rocks and reefs, and other ships. One of the most treacherous journeys is that around Cape Horn. This most southern point of South America juts out into Drake Passage – a narrow sea connecting the Atlantic and Pacific oceans. Fierce storms are common and the sea is always cold. The Dutch sailor, Willem Cornelis Schouten, was the first to sail around the Cape in 1616. In the great days of sailing, this journey was an all-important link between the Pacific and the Atlantic, and hundreds of ships were wrecked attempting it. Today, the lighthouse at Cape Horn (*above right*) marks a largely uninhabited area, and plays a crucial role.

One of the first lighthouses was built in 280 BC at Alexandria in Egypt, to guide sailors journeying across the Mediterranean Sea. Lighthouses have been used ever since to guide ships in storms and to help the crew avoid hidden rocks. Sometimes people called wreckers used to light beacons on cliff tops. Thinking that they were lighthouses, sailors would take the wrong course and crash against the rocks, leaving the cargo to be looted by the wreckers. Today's lighthouses are equipped with foghorns and radio beacons to help ships navigate safely in all weathers.

Deep waters

"Delivered from gravity, I flew around in space..." *Jacques Cousteau, diver*

Deep waters are among the most dangerous places in the world. There is little or no light and the pressure from the water is too great for the human body to stand – an unprotected diver (*right*) would be crushed.

Diving suits, such as the NEWTSUIT (*left*), allow people to explore the depths, and are also used in rescue situations. In emergencies, a range of special rescue vessels is used. Submersibles are mini-submarines which can transfer emergency supplies to the crews of damaged submarines, and can rescue crew members if necessary. 'Hyperbaric chambers' bring injured deep-sea divers to the surface at a steady pressure: if they ascend too quickly, they can suffer from a potentially fatal illness called 'the bends'.

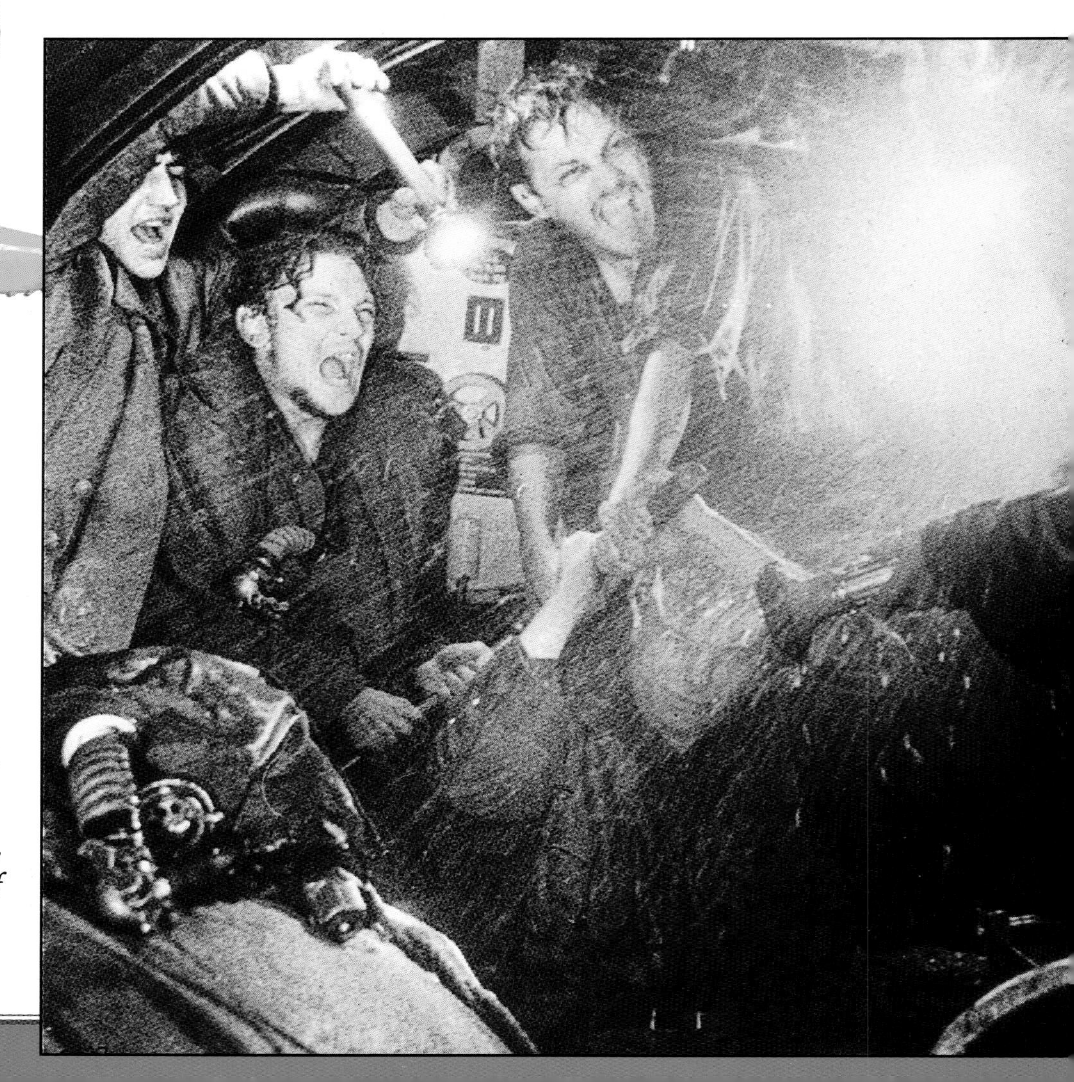

SUBMARINE TERROR

When a submarine is hit by a depth-charge or torpedo, water rushes in uncontrollably. There is nothing that can be done except seal off the affected areas and hope that the weight of the water does not stop the 'sub' rising to the surface. The television series Das Boot *(The Boat,* right*) showed the terror of German sailors in a submarine under attack.*

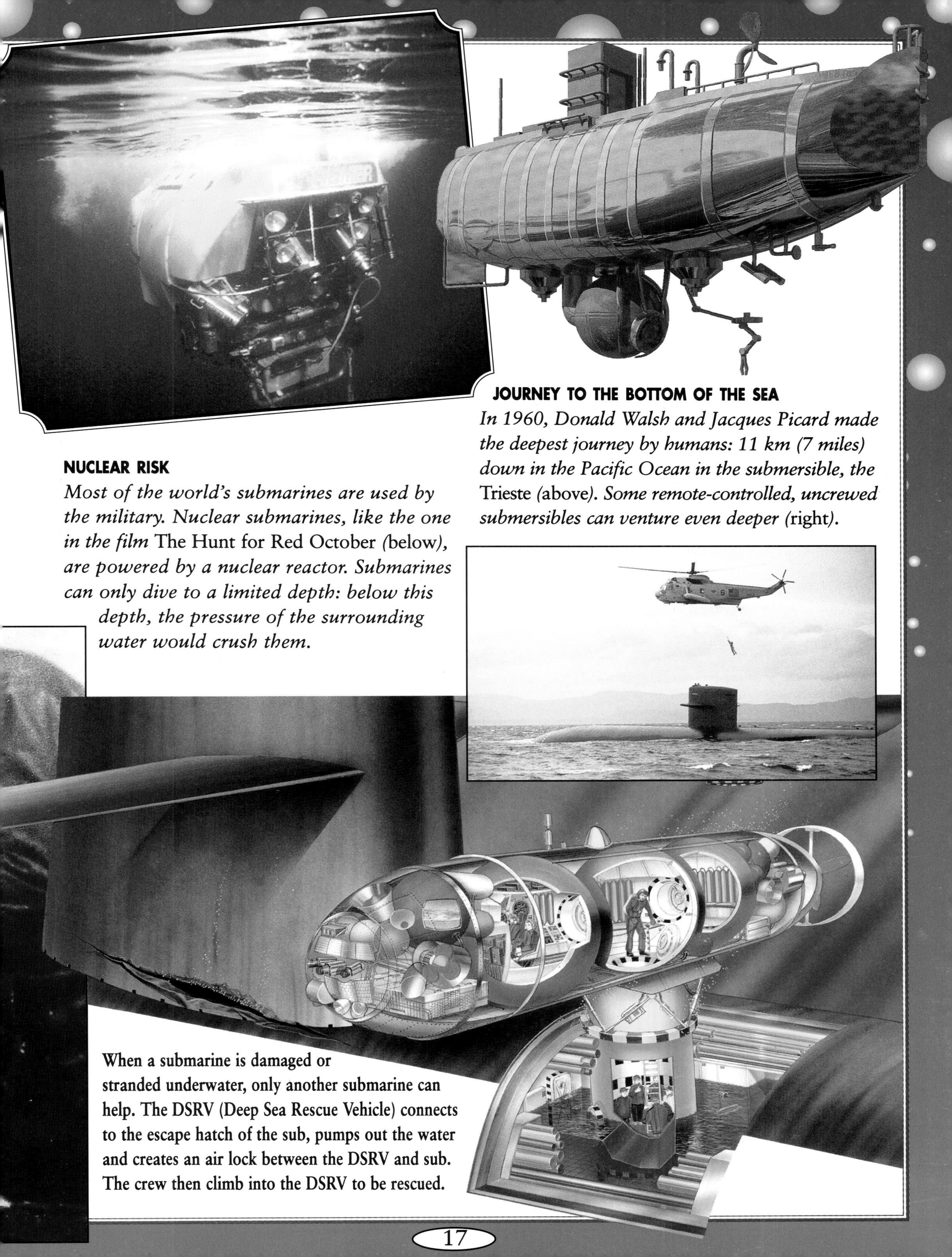

JOURNEY TO THE BOTTOM OF THE SEA

In 1960, Donald Walsh and Jacques Picard made the deepest journey by humans: 11 km (7 miles) down in the Pacific Ocean in the submersible, the Trieste *(*above*). Some remote-controlled, uncrewed submersibles can venture even deeper (*right*).*

NUCLEAR RISK

Most of the world's submarines are used by the military. Nuclear submarines, like the one in the film The Hunt for Red October *(*below*), are powered by a nuclear reactor. Submarines can only dive to a limited depth: below this depth, the pressure of the surrounding water would crush them.*

When a submarine is damaged or stranded underwater, only another submarine can help. The DSRV (Deep Sea Rescue Vehicle) connects to the escape hatch of the sub, pumps out the water and creates an air lock between the DSRV and sub. The crew then climb into the DSRV to be rescued.

Tsunamis

“The wave, like an enormous hand crumpling a long sheet of paper, crushed the houses one by one.” *Eye-witness,* tsunami *in Chile, 1960*

In 1960, an earthquake in Chile started a *tsunami* that swept across the Pacific to Japan. Huge waves washed over many coastal towns, destroying 50,000 houses and killing hundreds of people.

Tsunamis are huge waves up to 30 m (100 ft) tall which are set off by underwater volcanoes (*right*) or earthquakes. Scientists use earthquake-monitoring devices called seismographs to predict when a *tsunami* will hit a particular coast.

The waves can travel at 800 km (480 miles) per hour and are devastating when they reach shallow water. They crash onto the land, washing people, animals, homes and cars away – no sea wall is high enough to stop them. The power of *tsunamis* is so great that, in 1692, one that hit Port Royal in Jamaica threw ships onto the tops of buildings. It is said to have moved mountains and created huge splits in the earth which swallowed people whole.

WHAT ARE *TSUNAMIS*?

Tsunamis *are often called tidal waves, although they are not caused by natural tides. The burst of energy from an earthquake or underwater volcano sets the sea in motion. If the waves reach shallow waters, they bunch up and become one huge – and highly destructive – wave.*

The Japanese artist Katsushika Hokusai (1760-1849) made this print in 1831. It shows a huge *tsunami* tossing boats around like matchsticks.

HOLDING BACK THE WAVES

Japan suffers from many earthquakes and a large number of storms from regular typhoons. These sea defences (right) are used to minimise the damage caused when tsunamis crash onto the shore and to help prevent flooding from storm surges (see page 23). When the sea hits the defences, the energy of the waves is reduced by the special shape of the blocks.

WAVE GOODBYE TO HOME

No, it didn't get there under its own steam – this steamer was swept into the Sumatran jungle by a huge tsunami. The tsunami occurred in 1883 after the Indonesian island of Krakatau was blown apart by a volcano. Waves 12 m (40 ft) high destroyed coastal villages on Java and Sumatra.

Huge waves form

Waves become closer and taller near shore

When the *tsunami* hits land, it sweeps away everything in its path

The earthquake forces part of the seabed upwards

BLESSINGS IN DISGUISE

*Monsoons regularly bring devastating storms and cause flooding in river areas. But these floods help to make the land more fertile (*left*). The failure or late arrival of the monsoon rains can reduce crop harvests.*

A man struggles through the monsoon rains in Ho Chi Minh City in Vietnam.

WHAT ARE MONSOONS?

Monsoons are strong winds that change direction at different seasons. They mainly occur over South and Southeast Asia. The southwest, or summer, monsoon usually brings very heavy rain in India and Southeast Asia, and is the dominant climate event of the area.

SINKING CITIES

Located on the eastern side of the Indian Ocean, Bangkok, the capital city of Thailand, suffers from the southwest monsoon winds during the summer. Most of the people live on the river and so are affected by the storms and rains. Inadequate drainage makes the problem worse. In this flooded city street, motorbikes and cars are having to struggle through flood water after the heavy rains.

Monsoons

"The monsoon rains bring a relief from the heat, but can cause massive devastation." ***Shopkeeper, India, 1997***

Every June in India, the monsoon comes, bringing rain for three months, and sometimes it is torrential. The flooding can be terrifying. Rivers burst their banks, power failures cause shops to close, and streets are turned into muddy, waist-high rivers. Many people suffer injuries from stepping on glass and other objects submerged in the water and there is a high risk from water-borne diseases. Yet, wherever possible, life goes on: Indians have got used to the monsoons. They build dams (*above right*) and huts with raised floors, and store food on high platforms. The floods bring boatmen, ready to carry people from door to door for a fee.

In some years these torrential rains turn into disaster. In these cases, the army and relief organisations try desperately to distribute food and medical supplies. But, such is the scale of monsoon floods in India and Bangladesh, that often they struggle to provide sufficient help and it can take weeks before the situation is brought under control.

Business as usual in Bangkok after the monsoon rains.

STORM-WRECKED COASTS: HURRICANE HUGO
*Hurricane Hugo was one of the worst hurricanes to hit America in recent times. In 1989, it swirled across the country, attacking the Virgin Islands and Puerto Rico (*below*) and devastating Charleston (*above*), one of the busiest ports on the southeast coast of the United States. It killed 50 people and caused four million dollars worth of damage.*

Tropical storms

"The people of Acapulco were not used to getting hurricanes and didn't know what to expect." ***Red Cross official, 1997***

A severe tropical storm – called a hurricane, cyclone, or typhoon, depending on where it occurs – is a roaring vortex of wind which moves across the sea at speeds of up to 360 km/h (220 mph). The winds are so strong that anything in their path risks being destroyed.

In October 1997, Hurricane Pauline hit the holiday resort of Acapulco, Mexico – a town unused to hurricanes. In some areas, 50 cm (20 in) of rain fell in less than 24 hours, causing massive flooding and mudslides. More than 400 people were killed. Relief workers struggled to reach the mountainous and remote areas which had felt the full force of the hurricane. Food, temporary housing, and even 20,000 comfort kits (including toothpaste and brushes) were rushed in, and the clean-up operation was immense. For weeks, people wore paper face masks to protect against clouds of brown dust caused by the dried mud scraped up among the debris.

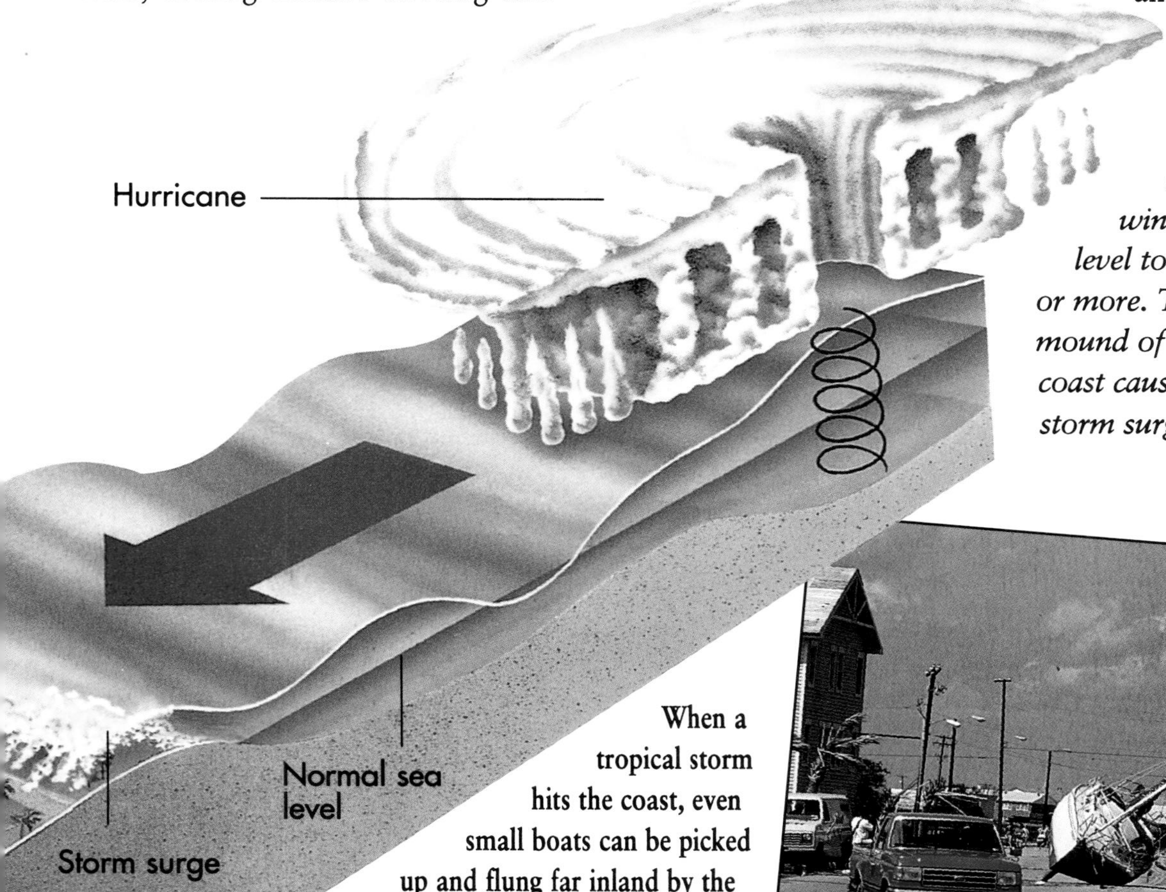

Hurricane

Normal sea level

Storm surge

STORM SURGE

*When a hurricane hits land, the fierce winds force the sea level to rise by 6 m (20 ft) or more. The winds wash a mound of water onto the coast causing a flood called a storm surge (*left*).*

When a tropical storm hits the coast, even small boats can be picked up and flung far inland by the hurricane's awesome power (*right*).

Droughts

"El Niño is continuing to evolve, continuing to be a very awesome event." ***Nick Green, Oceanologist, 1997***

Too little water can be as disastrous as too much. A lack of water is called a drought. In times of drought (*right*), people and animals die of thirst and crops wither, causing famines that can kill millions of people even in areas far away from the affected region. Wars and deforestation can make droughts worse – without trees, the soil cannot retain nearly as much moisture.

In 1997, a weather phenomenon began brewing in the Pacific Ocean. Called 'El Niño', it is a warming of the equatorial Pacific off South America which causes unusual changes in the climate around the world. This may well be the largest climatic event of the century, responsible for violent weather and droughts in Brazil, Africa, Australia and even the United States. In Indonesia, where the weather had been unusually dry, the farmers and logging companies continued to clear forests by burning trees, setting fire to large parts of the country.

The El Niño in 1993 to 1994 was not severe but, the one in August 1983, caused global damage estimated at £17 billion. High winds and heavy rains in the Arizona desert in the United States turned streets into rivers and toppled power lines.

The worst drought-related famine occurred in China in 1876-78, when 13 million people died. As people starved, roving bands of human skeletons searched for food (*above*). Travellers were killed and desperate parents sold their children as food (*above top*).

RAIN-SHADOW ZONES

*Droughts are usually caused by too little rainfall. Water travels between the land, seas and air in a never-ending circle called the water cycle. Heat from the sun turns water from the seas, lakes and rivers into vapour, which rises and forms clouds and rain. When clouds are lifted over mountains (*left*), rainfall is increased, leaving little on the other side of the mountain – a 'rain shadow'. Droughts can occur in these areas.*

A farmer in Mauritania, where water is scarce.

LIFE-GIVING WATER

The water in this pipe is usually reserved for watering crops. Here, in a time of drought, it provides a much-needed drink for a farmer. This is Mauritania, a country in western Africa, mostly covered by the Sahara desert. Intensive farming and clearing of scrubland causes desert areas to spread. Droughts get worse, and people flee from the drought stricken countryside into overcrowded urban areas.

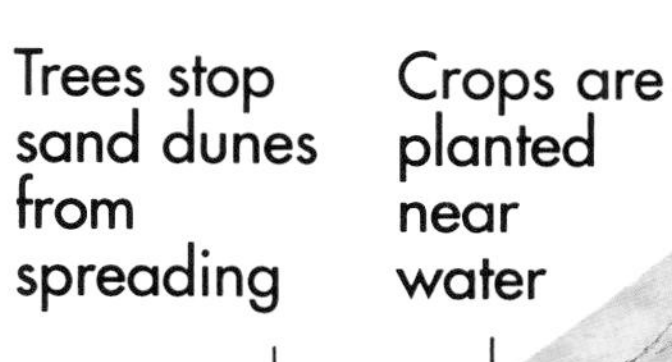

WHAT CAN BE DONE?

*There are a number of ways of reducing the effects of droughts (*right*). Dams can be built across rivers, providing reservoirs of water for irrigation and drinking. Trees are grown to hold the soil together and bring up water from deep in the ground. Terracing prevents the run off of rainwater and soil from hilly areas. The ancient system of building ditches and canals (*left*) is still used in many areas.*

KEEPING WATER IN

These dry stone walls in Mauritania are not to keep animals from wandering. They are built by labourers to function as dams around fields, to prevent soil from wearing away (erosion) and to trap in much-needed rainwater.

Frozen waters

"The decks broke up, the great beams snapping with a noise like gunfire." *Ernest Shackleton, Antarctica, 1914*

The freezing waters around Antarctica can be treacherous. In summer, the seas are dotted with large chunks of floating ice (*right*) and, in winter, the water's surface freezes into one continuous sheet of ice.

Here, one of the most incredible real-life adventures took place. In 1914, Irish explorer Ernest Shackleton was sailing through the Weddell Sea, a large gulf that cuts into mainland Antarctica. Without warning, huge sheets of ice crushed his ship, smashing its beams like matchsticks. The 28-strong crew were forced to abandon ship and set up camp on the drifting ice, but gale-force winds soon ripped their tents to shreds. Existing on penguin meat and seaweed, food supplies soon became scarce and Shackleton was forced to lead his crew on an extraordinary trek over frozen seas to Elephant Island, a tiny land mass about 1,000 km (620 miles) below South America. Leaving some men there, he continued with five others to South Georgia Island where, after a journey of almost 2,880 km (1,800 miles), he finally reached a whaling station. The station's commander who had seen them off two years before, now no longer recognised them as they looked so wild. All 28 crew were rescued.

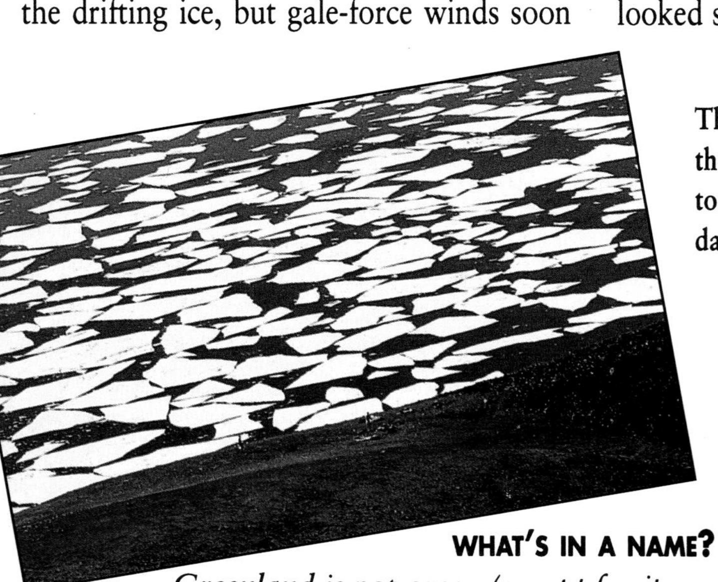

The sinking of the *Titanic* prompted the setting up of a special Ice Patrol to warn ships of potentially dangerous icebergs.

WHAT'S IN A NAME?

*Greenland is not green (except for its coastal areas in summer), and about 85 per cent of its 'land' is covered by ice (*above*). The country was named by Viking explorers who wished to attract settlers. Natives sail in narrow canoe-like boats which are the ideal shape for working their way through broken-up ice.*

This boat sails between floating ice in Arctic waters (*above*). If a boat gets stuck, rescue boats called ice-breakers may have to come to cut it free.

ARCTIC ACCIDENT-ZONES

*Icebergs are dangerous because they are so solid and most of their immense size is hidden beneath the water (*below*). Besides icebergs, the other main danger for ships in arctic waters is floating pack ice. If a ship gets stuck working its way through the huge broken sheets (*left*), it can be crushed to pieces as the ice pushes against it.*

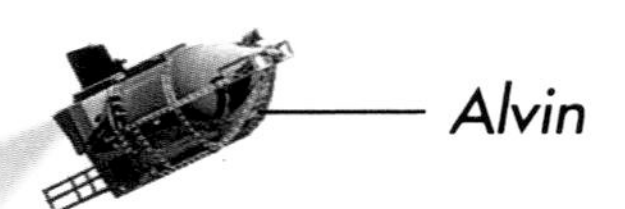

THE WRECK OF THE *TITANIC*

In 1986, the murky depths of the north Atlantic Ocean were spot-lit by bright beams from the small, three-person submersible, Alvin *(*left*). As the mud clouds cleared, a dark shape appeared. It was the bow of the* Titanic. *In 1912, this ocean liner had sunk in just three hours when it hit an iceberg on its first voyage across the Atlantic. Of the 2,220 people on board, more than 1,500 died. Many of these drowned in the icy, black waters as there were only enough lifeboats for half of the passengers.*

Weird water

"It was a terrible dark elephant grey, of a loathsome texture." *First sighting of the Loch Ness monster, 1933*

For centuries, the power of water has been a source of fascination and so it is no surprise to find countless stories and legends about this vital element.

For most of us, the oceans are as much of a mystery today as they were to the ancient sailors who told stories of sea gods and monsters to explain storms and shipwrecks. Even now, we are still excited by reported sightings of the Loch Ness monster. Perhaps one of the most enduring legends is that of the city of Atlantis whose ruins are believed to lie in the ocean's depths since being engulfed by waves in ancient times. There is no proof that Atlantis ever existed, yet searches for it continue.

From swirling whirlpools to the hot, bubbling waters of geysers (*left*), people have always been intrigued by weird and wonderful watery phenomena. But water is also claimed to have great healing power. Many ill people visit the holy spring at Lourdes in France, where the water is believed to heal the incurable.

LEGENDARY BEASTS

Whirlpools are a danger to small ships, which can get sucked down. A Greek myth tells of the monster Charybdis *(*left*), which swallowed and spat out the water of the sea three times a day. Loch Ness in Scotland is the home of the legendary Loch Ness monster (*right*). Hundreds of people claim to have seen it, although there is no evidence to prove that what they have seen really is a monster.*

THE ULTIMATE SEA VIEW?

For a holiday with a difference, you could check into the world's first underwater hotel in Florida, in the United States (above). *It is furnished with bedrooms, kitchens and living areas – all 9 m (30 ft) under the sea, and with views of the underwater world just outside the window. Guests can go on safaris into the open sea, straight from the hotel door.*

The 1995 film *Waterworld* is a story about the Earth being drowned by rising sea levels (*below*), and how the survivors adapt to the new conditions. Some scientists believe that sea levels will rise if global warming melts the icecaps. This could mean that parts of some low-lying countries, like Holland and Bangladesh, would disappear. We might well have to learn to live underwater!

Whilst the deepest parts of the ocean remain unexplored, legends persist. In the 1989 film, *The Abyss* (*above*), aliens lurked in the depths .

Emergency first-aid

Here is some practical advice for what to do in emergencies involving water.

Drowning

Drowning is a form of suffocation. The supply of air to the lungs is cut off completely by water. This cut-off does not create an immediate lack of oxygen in the body. There is a small reserve in the lungs and in the blood which can sustain life for up to six minutes or longer at low temperatures.

- A victim of drowning should be removed from the water as quickly as possible.
- Emergency services should be called immediately.
- If there is someone trained in first-aid present, he or she should begin artificial respiration. If not, wait for the emergency services to arrive.

Hypothermia

Hypothermia is the cooling of the entire body to dangerous levels. First, the victim will shiver, then he or she will become drowsy, before eventually falling unconscious.

- Get the victim out of the elements (wind, rain, snow, cold, etc.)
- Remove all wet clothing.
- Wrap the victim in blankets, making sure that the blankets are under, as well as over, the victim.
- To keep the victim warm, build a fire or place heat packs, electric heating pads, hot water bottles, or even another rescuer in the blankets with the victim. **Do not warm the victim too quickly.**
- Get the victim to a medical facility as soon as possible.

Glossary

Air pressure The weight of the atmosphere.

Atmosphere The layer of gases that surrounds the Earth. It is mostly nitrogen and oxygen, together with a little carbon dioxide and water vapour.

Atom The smallest particles, or 'building blocks', that make up all matter.

Cyclone A tropical storm that occurs in the Indian Ocean. It is also a wind circulation turning anti-clockwise in the northern hemisphere.

Dam A barrier that blocks the flow of a river.

Deforestation Cutting down most of the trees in a forest area.

Desert An area that has very little rainfall and few plants and animals.

Dike A wall made of earth, sand and stones to hold back water.

Drought A disaster caused by a lack of rainfall over a long period of time.

El Niño A change in equatorial Pacific Ocean temperatures which affects the world's climatic patterns.

Equatorial Refers to areas near the equator (the imaginary line that passes round the middle of the globe, halfway between the North and South poles).

Famine A disaster in which many people starve because of lack of food.

Fertile land Land that has all the elements that plants need in order to grow well.

Geyser A spring which throws up hot water from time to time, with explosive force.

Global warming A gradual increase in average global temperature. Global warming is possibly caused by a build-up of 'greenhouse gases' (mainly carbon dioxide), which trap more of the Sun's heat in the atmosphere.

Gravity A force of attraction which exists in all particles of matter, pulling them together. It keeps all things, including the atmosphere, attached to the Earth.

Hurricane The name for a severe tropical storm in the Atlantic Ocean.

Hydroelectric power Electricity made by using water pressure in a turbine to drive an electric generator.

Irrigation Watering of crops by channels from a river or reservoir.

Monsoon An wind in Asia that changes with the seasons. It can bring heavy rainfall.

Reservoir A lake used for storing water.

Sea defences High walls or concrete blocks on a coast that stop sea water flooding the land.

Silt Fine-grained sand or mud which settles in water.

Submersible Small craft, similar to a submarine, that can travel to great depths underwater.

Terracing Steps dug into land on slopes to prevent soil being washed downhill.

Trench A deep valley on the sea floor.

Tsunami A huge wave caused by movement of the seabed after an earthquake or underwater volcano.

Typhoon The name for a severe topical storm that occurs in the China seas and West Pacific area.

Volcano An opening in the Earth's surface, either on land or underwater, through which gases and molten rock from inside the Earth erupt.

Vortex A swirling mass of air or water.

Water cycle The recycling of water from the seas, into the air as clouds, and back into the rivers as rain.

Index

Picture Credits

(t-top, m-middle, b-bottom, r-right, l-left)

Front cover ml, 6bl, 19b, 23t: Mary Evans Picture Library; Front cover mr, 4-5, 5b, 6-7, 7 both, 8-9 all, 10 both, 11tr 11b, 12 both, 13t, 14-15 all, 17 both, 19t, 20-21 all, 22 both, 23b, 24mr, 25 both, 26 both, 27t, 28-29 all, 30, 31: Frank Spooner Pictures; Front cover b, 18t: Rex Features; 11tl, 24ml: Hulton Getty; 13b: Ealing Studios Courtesy Kobal Collection; 16: Bavaria/Radiant Courtesy Kobal Collection, 18b: The Bridgeman Art Library; 28: James Davis Travel.